# About the Author

Like most mothers she enjoyed cooking with her children and over the years of all of them being covered in flour, having messy worktops and success and failures from the cooker her children are now grown up and able to cook for themselves.

# Dedication

To my children for the inspiration they gave to me around the kitchen. As over the years of cooking together this has enabled me to create the Beginners Cookbook. Not forgetting my suffering husband Steve for eating my cooking with not too much complaining.

# K. Mortimer

# BEGINNERS COOKBOOK

AUSTIN MACAULEY
PUBLISHERS LTD.

A CIP catalogue record for this title is available from the British Library.

ISBN 9781786123848 (Paperback)
ISBN 9781786123855 (Hardback)
ISBN 9781786123862 (E-Book)

www.austinmacauley.com

First Published (2017)
Austin Macauley Publishers Ltd.
25 Canada Square
Canary Wharf
London
E14 5LQ

# Acknowledgments

To everyone who wants to start cooking and has thought it too time consuming and complicated, this cookery book has been compiled using simple and straightforward recipes.

You will find no gourmet recipes in here. It will only be the quick and easiest way to make something edible. Quick, relating to the preparation time rather than the cooking time. It is aimed at someone leaving home for the first time to which a cooker is a stranger or a student who has suddenly got to feed themselves or even someone who has never cooked before, but has decided to give it a go. I once met a man of 87 whose wife had died suddenly. He had never had to cook, but as he still wanted to eat, he had to learn.

You may feel that some of my comments are a bit obvious, but please remember that not everyone knows as much as you do and they may appreciate it. If not, I can only apologise.

# Contents

# HINTS AND TIPS

Those of an electric oven is the same temperature all over, whilst a gas one is the temperature you set it to in the middle, it is hotter at the top and cooler at the bottom. The equivalent temperatures are as follows: -

| Gas | Electric Centigrade | Electric Fahrenheit |
|---|---|---|
| 1 | 140 | 275 |
| 2 | 150 | 300 |
| 3 | 160 | 325 |
| 4 | 180 | 350 |
| 5 | 190 | 375 |
| 6 | 200 | 400 |
| 7 | 220 | 425 |
| 8 | 230 | 450 |
| 9 | 240 | 475 |

A wooden spoon should be used when stirring food on top of the oven so the heat doesn't travel along and burn your hand. It is best to use one spoon for savoury and another for sweet, as it adopts the flavour, and onion flavoured rice pudding isn't a favourite.

All onions I use are Spanish onions. Any onion can be used but you will probably need a whole onion rather than half, as they tend to be smaller. Do not forget to remove the dry brown skin before you start to chop it.

Spoon measurements are easier. If you are short of spoons, 2 teaspoons equals 1 dessertspoon, 2 dessertspoons equals 1 tablespoon.

Any pepper used is normally black pepper, but the type doesn't really matter. You are only interested in the flavour.

Many vegetables are pre-washed nowadays, so it is up to you whether you decide to peel or not.

You can mix the recipes however you want to. You can do it by hand, by mixer or food processor. It's just harder work for you if you do it by hand.

If you don't like something in the recipe, just change it to something you do like. You should try the recipe first though, because you often can't taste all the ingredients.

If the fumes from onions get in your eyes, try wearing sunglasses when you chop them. It may help a little.

Once you can deal with the recipes in this book, you are ready to be a professional chef.

# BREAKFAST

Putting an egg in a saucepan and adding boiled water can make soft-boiled eggs. Turn the gas high and bring it back to the boil. Then turn the gas down to simmer and time it for 3 minutes. Then it's ready. For a hard-boiled egg time it for 12 minutes.

Toast can be made one of two ways, by putting it in the toaster or by grilling it. You just put sliced bread in the toaster, choose the colour you would like it to be (best to start with medium). Put the bread down using the appropriate button and when it's ready it will pop up. To grill it put the slices of bread on the grill and turn it on. When it's toasted on one side turn it over and toast the other side. This side will cook a lot more quickly. Spread butter or margarine on the toast and then you can add a favourite topping like jam or marmalade.

To make beans on toast, just warm up a small tin of beans, or half a medium sized tin, in a saucepan. Turn on to a medium heat. When they're warm, pour over the toast. It's best to put leftover beans in a covered pot in the fridge.

To make scrambled eggs just break an egg into a mug. Use a fork to mix it. Then pour it into a saucepan or frying pan. Put the pan onto a high heat and stir constantly with a wooden spoon (to stop the heat travelling up the spoon and burning your fingers.) It should take two or three minutes and then it will be ready. Pour it on toast or eat with a cooked breakfast. It would probably be better to put water in the pan when you've finished, because it will be difficult to clean otherwise.

Porridge isn't difficult to make. Just put 300ml of milk into a saucepan with 1 cup of porridge oats. Put on the hob with a medium heat. Use a wooden spoon to stir constantly, until the mixture thickens. It's now ready. You can also cook it in a microwave. Put the milk and porridge oats into a bowl. Cook for 2 minutes on a high heat and then stir. Cook for a further 1½ minutes then it is ready.

A fried breakfast can be made without using a lot of oil, if you use a non-stick pan. You will need to cook sausages and/or bacon first so that any fat coming from the meat will line the pan. If you use a normal frying pan you will first need to put in about 2 tablespoons full of cooking oil. Prick any sausages first to stop them bursting out of their skins. When you are cooking a breakfast, only cook the amount of everything you want to eat. It sounds obvious but it is likely to be wasted otherwise. Start with the bacon and sausages on a medium heat and cook until the colour changes. Make sure the sausage is properly cooked for long enough because you don't want food poisoning. Then put that in the oven on a low heat whilst everything else cooks. Then you could cook the mushrooms. First wipe them clean, cut them in half and cook in the pan until brown. Tomatoes can be cooked by cutting them in half first. They are likely to only take a couple of minutes. Beans should be cooked in a separate saucepan. Fried bread should be cut in half before being placed in the pan. It will need 2 or 3 minutes to cook but will soak up all the oil, so you may need to add extra. Eggs should be left until last, as they don't take long to cook. Only about 2 or 3 minutes. You will need to put a little more oil in to fry them. Some people prefer them turned over so cook them how you like them best. Crack the egg on the side of the pan and open it out in the middle. Then start frying.

# MAIN MEALS

# CHILLI CON CARNE

**YOU NEED**

1 tin of tomatoes
1 tin of red kidney beans
Half a kg (1lb) minced beef
Half an onion
Chilli powder
1 tablespoon oil

**TO MAKE**

Chop the onion quite small. Put it in a saucepan with some oil and cook until soft. Stir from time to time with a wooden spoon. Alternatively, if a microwave is available, you can put the onion in a bowl in the microwave. Cook for 3 minutes and you will reach the same stage. Put the onion in a casserole dish. Add the minced beef. Open the tin of tomatoes. Put a knife in and roughly chop the tomatoes. Add them to the casserole dish. Open the tin of beans. Put them in a sieve and wash them. If you don't have a sieve, cover the beans with the lid and empty out the fluid. Add water to the tin and empty that out. Repeat once, and then tip the beans into the casserole dish. Finally, the chilli powder is to be added. It is wise to check the strength of the powder first. A hot powder may only need a teaspoonful, whereas a mild powder may need a dessert spoonful. If you don't check, you could find that the chilli is too hot to eat, as I know from personal experience. Stir then cook on the middle shelf, gas mark 5, for 1 hour or if you prefer gas mark 3 for 2 hours. It is best to stir it after the first hour to try to prevent it from going into clumps.
This will feed 4 people so you will need access to a few good friends or a fridge or freezer.
If you really don't like red beans, you can try substituting them with baked beans to see if you like it any better. This

would normally be eaten with salad or rice – scc Chickcn curry.

# SPAGHETTI BOLOGNAISE

**YOU NEED**

Half an onion
Half a kg (1lb) minced beef
1 tin of tomatoes
4 button mushrooms
2 bay leaves
Sprinkle oregano or basil
1 tablespoon of oil

**TO MAKE**

Chop the onion and put in a large saucepan with the oil. Fry using a wooden spoon to stir as it cooks. You can also do it by putting the onion in a bowl for 3 minutes in a microwave oven. Add the minced beef. Wipe the mushrooms then slice them thinly and add to the pan. Open the tin of tomatoes and insert a knife into the tin. Roughly chop the tomatoes and add to the pan. The bay leaves should then be added with the oregano or basil. This should then be cooked, starting with a high heat then reducing to simmer for 45 minutes.
When cooked, remove the bay leaves before serving. This will serve 4 people or you could save some for another meal (e.g. lasagne).
To cook the spaghetti, you will need about half a packet. Put it in a large saucepan with boiling water to half fill the pan. Start by turning the heat full on, and then reduce it once it starts boiling. It will take about 12 minutes to cook. When ready strain before serving. If you don't have a strainer, hold the lid on the saucepan as you empty the water out.

# CHICKEN CURRY

**YOU NEED**

Half an onion
Half a kg (1lb) chicken – raw or pre cooked
1 kg (2lb) potatoes
Half a kg (1lb) of carrots
1 tin of tomatoes
Curry powder
2 tablespoons oil
2 dessertspoons plain flour

**TO MAKE**

Chop the onion and put it in a large saucepan with the oil.
Fry the onion whilst stirring with a wooden spoon. If using a
microwave, put the onion in a jug or bowl and put in the
microwave for 3 minutes. Put on a medium heat. Cut the
chicken into pieces about 5cm (2 inches) in area. Add to the
onion. Add the curry powder after reading the instructions
on the packet to make sure you put the right amount in. If
you are not sure how strong you want it, you are probably
best to start with madras. If you know you like it hot, try a
tandoori or even hotter. Open the tin of tomatoes. Put a knife
in and chop the tomatoes a little smaller. Then tip them into
the saucepan. Peel the potatoes and chop into medium sized
pieces. Peel the carrots and cut them into slices or lengths,
whichever you prefer. The potatoes and carrots then go into
the saucepan which is filled with boiling water to cover the
vegetables. In a cup put the flour with a little cold water. Stir
well, and then add to the pan. Stir the whole contents of the
pan. Turn the heat up until it boils and then turn it down
again. It should take 1 to 1 and half hours to cook and should
serve 3 to 4 people.
You can change to whichever meat you want, or if it's a
vegetarian curry you prefer just add extra vegetables. If you

wish to, you can also have a curried egg by adding a hard boiled egg half an hour before the end of cooking. Look at Breakfast for how to make a hard-boiled egg. This will allow time for the curry flavour to be taken up by the egg.

# RICE

Place a large cup of rice in a saucepan. Pour on plenty of boiling water. Turn the heat up high to bring back to the boil, then turn down to simmer. Allow 10 minutes for white rice to cook, 15 for brown. When it has cooked, put it in a sieve to strain out the water. If you wish you can serve straight away or wash out the starch under cold running water. You will then need to put it in a dish in the oven, gas mark 5, and middle shelf for 30 minutes to warm up.

This will serve 1-2 people.

# MACARONI CHEESE

Making the cheese sauce is more involved than cooking the macaroni. In a large saucepan put 100g (4 oz) macaroni. Add boiling water to fill the pan to about 5cm (about 2 inches) above the macaroni. Bring to the boil then turn down to simmer for 12 minutes. You will need to make the cheese sauce whilst this is cooking.

To make a CHEESE SAUCE you will need
25g (1 oz) butter
50g (2 oz) plain flour
75g (3 oz) grated cheese
Half a pint of milk
Salt and pepper

**TO MAKE**

Put the butter in a saucepan, put the heat on low and melt it. Add the flour and stir together. In another pan boil the milk. Add the milk to the flour mixture. Add the cheese, salt and pepper and mix with a wooden spoon. Turn up the heat and stir, until the milk boils and the mixture thickens. Then turn the heat off and leave on one side. Empty the water out of the macaroni either by putting it into a sieve or by putting the lid on and draining the water out. Fill a dish with the macaroni and cover with the cheese sauce. Give it a quick stir to make sure it is all covered.
This will serve 1 person.
You can use whatever kind of pasta you wish if you don't like macaroni or fancy a change.

# LASAGNE

**YOU NEED**

About 150 (6 oz) Bolognaise sauce (see spaghetti bolognaise)
About half a pint of cheese sauce (see macaroni cheese)
Lasagne sheets
50g (2 oz) grated cheese

**TO MAKE**

In a dish, put half the bolognaise sauce. Lay a sheet of lasagne on top, and then put on half of the cheese sauce. Repeat once. Sprinkle the grated cheese on the top. Put in the middle of the oven on gas mark 5 for 30 minutes or until it's cooked. If you would prefer a vegetable Lasagne, put in some vegetables e.g. 1 sliced carrot, 1 medium potato cut into small pieces, 1 sliced courgette, 1 handful of peas and 1 sliced mushroom. Put the vegetables in a saucepan with some cold water. Turn the heat high until it boils, and then turn down to a simmer for 20 minutes. When it is cooked put the lid on and drain out the water. Add 1 sliced tomato. Replace the bolognaise sauce in the recipe with vegetables for a vegetarian dish.
If the dish is about the same size as 1 sheet of Lasagne it will feed 1-2 people.

# SPANISH OMELETTE

**YOU NEED**

5 tablespoons oil
2 rings of red pepper
1 mushroom
1 tomato
1 spring onion
A handful of peas
2 eggs

**TO MAKE**

Put 2 tablespoons of the oil in a frying pan. Cut the pepper into small pieces. Wipe the mushroom and slice that too, throwing away the end of the mushroom. Peel the dirty outer leaves of the spring onion, chop the root end off and then cut (including the green part) into slices. Cut the tomato in half and then turn and slice lengthways. Put the peas in the pan with the other vegetables. Turn the pan on to a hot heat and start cooking. Spread the vegetables over the bottom of the pan. Break the eggs into a jug and whisk with a fork. Add the rest of the oil to the pan. Pour the eggs into the frying pan. Cook for about 3 minutes or until the eggs have set. It is then ready.
This will serve 1 person.

# SHEPHERDS PIE

**YOU NEED**

Half an onion
1 tablespoon oil
Half a kg (1lb) minced lamb
1 dessertspoon mint sauce
2 dessertspoons gravy powder or a beef stock cube
Half pint cold water
2 large potatoes
25g (1 oz) butter
A little milk

**TO MAKE**

Cut the onion into slices and then small pieces. Into a large sized saucepan put the onion and oil. Cook on a medium heat and stir occasionally with a wooden spoon. Add the minced lamb. Into a jug, put cold water and stir in the gravy powder or crumbled stock cube. It should then be put in the saucepan with the minced lamb and the mint sauce should be added. Stir well from time to time.

Next, you need to peel the potatoes and cut them into medium to small sized pieces. Put them into another saucepan with enough cold water to cover them. Turn up to boil then down to simmer. They should take about 25 minutes to cook. Once it has cooked, add the milk and butter. Mash them with a potato masher. If you haven't got one you can use a fork, but it will take a long time. Get out a heatproof mat and put a dish on it. Empty the contents of the mince pan into it. Top this with the mashed potatoes then put the dish in the oven on the middle shelf, gas mark 5. Warm for 30 minutes.

This will serve 2 to 4 people. If you decide to use minced beef instead of lamb (and don't include mint sauce) you will have made cottage pie.

# CHICKEN DINNER

**YOU NEED**

1½ kg (3lb) chicken

**TO COOK**

First you will need to remove the wrapping from the chicken and the giblets pack from inside its body. In larger chickens it is sometimes put in the neck end, so check first before cooking. Cook in a pre-heated oven, gas mark 5, for 2½ to 3 hours.

Some people fry the giblets in 2 tablespoons of oil to eat or use in other ways, e.g. gravy, but I just throw them away.

To check that a chicken is cooked, prick it. If the juices that come out are clear, it's ready, if not leave for another 30 minutes before you try again.

Most fresh vegetables should be put in cold water to cook, brought to the boil on a high heat, then turned down to simmer for 25 minutes.

Peel vegetables like carrots or parsnips, cut the tops and bottoms off and throw away. Cut into circles or strips then cook. Potatoes should be peeled and cut into medium sized pieces. Brussels should have any dried or damaged leaves removed and cut off the end of the stalk. A small cross should be cut into the stalk end to allow the water to penetrate. When cooking cabbage, first cut the cabbage in half. Remove any dried or damaged leaves and trim the stalk. Cut the half, across the width, into strips not more than 2cm (1 inch) wide.

If you like cauliflower, break off the florets so that they are no more than 5cm (2 inches) wide. You can eat the leaves, but you are best to remove them from the stalk first. Just cut them into smallish pieces, remove the stalk and cook.

With frozen or tinned vegetables you need to put them into a saucepan and cover with boiling water. Put on the stove on a high heat, turning down to simmer once boiling. Cook for 5 minutes. Then it will be ready.

Half a teaspoon of salt put in the water when you cook the vegetables will improve the flavour. If you are avoiding salt, you can try using a splash of vinegar or soy sauce.

You can roast potatoes or parsnips by putting them, raw, in a roasting dish about 20cm x 15cm by 3cm deep (8 x 6 by 1½ inches deep). Make sure that all the potatoes are covered in oil. You can cook them with the chicken if you prefer, it will add a little flavour. Cooked separately, you need to put them in the oven 1 or 2 shelves underneath the chicken for 1 to 1½ hours. Using about 7 tablespoons of oil. Spoon fat over them every now and again. Once the potatoes are cooked you can put them at the bottom of the oven until everything else is ready. If you decide to cook the potatoes without the chicken, it is the middle shelf, gas mark 5, for 1 to 1½ hours. You can cook stuffing with the potatoes. To 1 packet of stuffing mix, add 1 egg and a little water. You can then form it into balls if you wish. They can be added to the pan you cook the potatoes in. As they only need about 45 minutes to cook, put them in a bit later.

To make a Yorkshire pudding you will need 2 rounded tablespoons of plain flour, 1 egg, and half a teaspoon of salt and enough cold water to mix to a cream-like consistency. Do not start cooking the vegetables or the Yorkshire pudding until the chicken has cooked. Once it has cooked you should take it out and put it on one side, preferably under a food net to keep out the flies. Make sure that the roast potatoes are at the bottom of the oven. Turn it up to gas mark 7. Put the Yorkshire pudding tin in the top of the oven with just oil in, to warm up for 5 minutes. You will need about 1 dessertspoon of oil for a Yorkshire pudding tin, 1 teaspoon if you use a small cake tin. When the oil is hot, quickly remove the tin. Pour in the Yorkshire pudding mixture and return it to the oven. It should be cooked in about 30 minutes.

To make gravy, either follow the instructions on the packet of gravy powder or add 2 tablespoons of plain flour to a jug and 2 crumbled stock cubes mixed with half a pint of cold water. Put in a saucepan and warm up by putting on a high heat then turning down to simmer, stirring constantly until it thickens. If you prefer thinner gravy, add extra water, thicker, add a little flour first mixed to a paste in a cup with a little water. The gravy is enough for 1 person, you need to make more to serve more people.

The meal will serve 1-4 people depending on how many vegetables you cook, how much you like Yorkshire pudding and how you cut the chicken. If you have access to a refrigerator you can slice one side of the breast for dinner (probably for 1 person), the other for sandwiches, two legs to eat with sandwiches and the rest of the meat off the chicken for a curry.

# BEEF CASSEROLE

**YOU NEED**

Half an onion
200g (8 oz) stewing steak
1 large potato
2 carrots
Half a tin of tomatoes
Salt and pepper
1 beef stock cube

**TO MAKE**

Cut the onion into slices and then into quarters. Put them in a casserole dish. Wash the steak and dab dry with some kitchen roll. If the steak is not already cut, slice into pieces no bigger than 5cm (2 inches) square. Peel the potato and cut into 8 pieces. Peel and slice the carrots, discarding the top and bottom. Put all the vegetables and the steak into the casserole dish. Put a knife in the tomato tin and chop them a bit smaller. Add to the casserole dish with the salt and pepper and the crumbled stock cub. Pour on boiling water to cover everything in the casserole dish. Put into an oven on the middle shelf, gas mark 5, for 30 minutes. Turn the oven down to gas mark 3 and cook for a further 2 hours. If the gravy is not thick enough, half an hour before you eat it, mix 1 dessertspoon of plain flour with a little water and add to the casserole.
This will serve 2 people.

# FISH AND CHIPS

**YOU NEED**

1 breaded fish piece
1 portion oven chips
1 large handful of peas

**TO MAKE**

Set the oven to gas mark 7. Put one shelf at the top of the oven, the other a rung or two lower down. Put the chips on a tray and put it on the top shelf. Put the fish on another tray and place on the lower shelf. Cook for 25-30 minutes. The peas should be put in a saucepan, and then filled with boiling water. Put on a high heat, and then lower to a simmer for 5 minutes.
This will serve one person.

# CHICKEN STIR-FRY

**YOU NEED**

1 pack of bean sprouts
2 mushrooms
2 spring onions
Half a red pepper
1 chicken breast
1 tomato
3 tablespoons of oil
Salt and pepper

**TO MAKE**

Wash the bean sprouts in a colander. Cut the chicken into thin strips. Wash the pepper and make sure all the seeds have been removed. Wipe the mushroom, cut and throw away the end of the stalk and cut into slices. Remove the outside of the spring onion and remove and throw away the end. Cut the rest (including the green part) into slices. Cut the tomato into slices and then strips. Put the oil into a wok or frying pan. Add all the vegetables and chicken and add the salt and pepper. Cook on a high heat for 3-5 minutes or until the chicken is cooked (turns white). To add a little more flavour you can add a little lemon juice. This will serve 1-2 people.

# SNACKS

# JACKET POTATO WITH CHEESE

**YOU NEED**

1 large potato
25g (1 oz) butter
50 g (2 oz) grated cheese

**TO MAKE**

Wash the potato under a tap to make sure it is clean. Prick all over with a fork. You only need to just break the surface, not puncture it. Put on a tray in the middle shelf, gas mark 6, for about an hour. A very big potato will need longer. When it is cooked, remove from the oven, put on a serving plate and cut in half. You can scrape it out and mash it before returning the potato to the skin, if you prefer. Add the butter and top with the cheese. It's then ready to eat and will serve 1.

# FRENCH ONION SOUP

**YOU NEED**

Half an onion
1 stock cube
1 tablespoon oil
1 slice of French bread

**TO MAKE**

Slice the onion and cut into quarters. Place in a saucepan with the oil. Put on a medium heat and fry, using a wooden spoon to stir. In a jug put half a pint of cold water. Add a crumbled stock cube and stir to mix in. Add to the saucepan. Turn up the heat to boil, and then turn down to simmer for 15 minutes. At the same time, toast the French bread on both sides. When the soup is ready, pour into a bowl and drop the French bread on the top.
This will serve 1 person.

# BARGAIN BURGERS

**YOU NEED**

200g (8 oz) minced beef
Half an onion
Half a packet of sage and onion stuffing mix
1 egg
2 tablespoons oil
4 baps

**TO MAKE**

Chop the onion into small pieces. Mix the egg and the stuffing together. Into a large bowl put the minced beef, onion and stuffing mix. Blend together, and then divide into 4. Roll each piece into a ball. Press the balls into a flatter, round shape. Hopefully, now they look like beef burgers. Put the oil into a frying pan. Add the beef burgers and fry until cooked. You should need to turn them once. When cooked, slice the baps open and put them in the baps. They are now ready to eat.

This makes 4 burgers, but you can make them smaller if you wish.

# HOT DOGS

**YOU NEED**

2 bread rolls
1 tablespoon oil
2 sausages
Half an onion (optional)

**TO MAKE**

Slice the onion. Cut the slices into quarters. Put the oil into the frying pan. Add the onion and prick the sausages. Add them to the frying pan. Turn on to a medium heat. Turn the sausage and onions regularly as they cook, to stop them burning. Slice the rolls almost in half (it doesn't matter from which direction). When the sausages are cooked, the colour will change before this happens, put one on each roll and add the onions. You may wish to add something like tomato sauce, mustard or salt and vinegar, before eating.
This will serve one person.

# TOAD IN THE HOLE

**YOU NEED**

4 sausages
2 tablespoons oil
2 tablespoons plain flour
1 egg
Half a teaspoon of salt

**TO MAKE**

Make sure you have a tin at least 5cm (1 inch) deep. Prick the sausage with a fork. Put the oil and sausage in the tin. Turn the oven to gas mark 6 and put the tin on a middle shelf for 30 minutes. Make the Yorkshire pudding mix by putting the flour, egg and salt in a jug with enough water to mix to the thickness of cream. Remove the sausage from the oven, turn it to number 7 and put them back on a high shelf for 5 minutes to bring the oil up to the right temperature. Take the tin out of the oven. Give the Yorkshire pudding mixture a quick whisk and pour it into the tin. Return to the top of the oven for 30 minutes. It should then be ready to eat. It would normally be served with vegetables and gravy (see chicken dinner) or chips (see fish and chips). This will serve 2 people.

# BACON FLIP

**YOU NEED**

1 packet puff pastry
2 slices bacon
100g (4 oz) grated cheese

**TO MAKE**

Thaw the pastry first. Sprinkle the worktop with flour. Rub flour on the rolling pin. Roll out the pastry with the rolling pin to about 30cm (12 inches) wide. Cut the pastry in half horizontally, then lengthways, so you should now have 4 squares of pastry. Cut the rind off of the bacon and then cut it into half lengthways. Turn the pastry squares to look like diamonds. Lay a strip of bacon lengthways on the pastry. Cover with the grated cheese. Flap the pastry over the bacon and cheese. On the half left, dab some water and press to the other piece of pastry to stick them together. Put on a tray, and then in the oven just above the middle shelf on gas mark 6 for 25-30 minutes.
This should be a treat for up to 4 people, but as it is popular in my house, it could be less.

# GARLIC BREAD

**YOU NEED**

1 baguette
75 g (3 oz) butter
3 good squirts of garlic puree (or paste)

**TO MAKE**

Place the butter in a bowl. It should be fairly soft, so try putting it in a microwave for 10 seconds or put it somewhere warm for a while. Then mix in the garlic puree.

Slice the baguette into pieces about 2cm (1 inch) thick. You should not cut it all the way through. Leave about 1cm (half an inch) at the bottom. Spread the butter on one side of each slice. Wrap the roll in foil and put it on a baking tray. Put it in the oven, middle shelf at gas mark 5, for 20 minutes. It should then be ready to eat.

It depends how much you like it how many people this will serve.

# PRAWN COCKTAIL

**YOU NEED**

4 large iceberg lettuce leaves. You will need more leaves if you use smaller ones
1 tomato
3cm or 1½ inch cucumber
2 spring onions
100g or 4 oz cooked prawns
2 dishes

**TO MAKE**

Slice the lettuce leaves. Slice and quarter the tomato and cucumber.
Remove the root of the spring onions and slice them too.
Add all of the salad ingredients to the dishes and sprinkle the prawns over the top.

**THE SAUCE**

2 dessert spoons of salad cream
Squirt of tomato ketchup
2 desert spoons of Tartar sauce
Paprika
Mix together the tartar sauce, salad cream and tomato sauce.
Spoon the sauce over the prawns and sprinkle a little Paprika over the top.
This will taste like a Marie Rose sauce which can be used on other fish dishes.

# SAUSAGE ROLLS

**YOU NEED**

1 packet of puff pastry
1 pack of sausage meat
Cayenne pepper (optional)
An egg (optional)

**TO MAKE**

Thaw the pastry first. Sprinkle some flour on the worktop. Rub flour into the rolling pin. Roll the pastry until it measures about 45cm (18 inches) by 30cm (12 inches). Slice it in half lengthways to make 2 long strips.

Cut the sausage meat in half and roll into two sausages about 45cm (18 inches) long. Now you have to decide whether to use Cayenne pepper or not. It will make the sausage rolls spicier. If so, sprinkle it on one side of the pastry. Lay the sausage meat on top of the pastry. With a pastry brush, brush water down one side of the pastry. Fold the pastry over the sausage meat and press down gently with your fingertips. With the blunt side of a knife, tap lightly along the joined edge of the pastry and it will encourage it to flake. Cut it into pieces about 8cm (3 inches) long. If you have some kitchen scissors, snip the sausage rolls twice on the top. Otherwise, prick them with a fork to let the steam out. Then crack an egg into a cup. Beat with a fork. Using a pastry brush, brush over the sausage rolls. If you do not want to use egg then do it with water.

Place them on a tray, then into an oven. Just above the middle shelf, gas mark 6, for 25-30 minutes. When you take them out, it's best to put them on a cooling rack for a while before eating, because they're a bit too hot.

# STUFFED PEPPERS

**YOU NEED**

3 peppers
1 pkt of vegetable rice
You may also need up to 3 tomatoes

**TO MAKE**

Slice the tops off the peppers 1 cm (½ inch) down and remove all of the seeds from the peppers and tops. Rinse the peppers and tops under a cold tap to remove any remaining seeds. Follow the packet of rice instructions and make it up.
Place the peppers into a tin so that they are upright and cannot fall over.
Carefully spoon the rice equally into the peppers and if they are not full, slice a tomato and put it on the top of the peppers.
Replace the tops of the peppers and put them into the oven on the middle shelf at gas mark 5 and cook for 25 minutes.
This will serve 3 people.

# DESSERTS

# PEACH FLAN

**YOU NEED**

1 flan tin
100g (4 oz) self-raising flour
100g (4 oz) caster sugar
100g (4 oz) soft margarine
1 teaspoon vanilla essence
2 eggs
1 tin of peach slices
1 packet quick setting jelly
1 glace cherry

**TO MAKE**

Grease the tin, particularly where the tin dips to form the flan shape. Cover this with a little flour to prevent a grease mark appearing on the flan. Using a food processor, mixer or just a mixing bowl to hand mix. Put the flour, caster sugar, soft margarine, vanilla essence and eggs into a bowl. Mix well until the mixture is thick and creamy. Put this in the tin and make it fairly level. Put the tin in the oven on the middle shelf, gas mark 5, for 30 minutes. To check that it is cooked, press gently in the middle with your finger. It should bounce back into place if it is cooked. If not, check again after 5 minutes. It shouldn't take much longer. Remove from the oven and put upside down on a cooling rack (sponge on the rack). This should make it easier to take it out of the tin when it has cooled. Use a pallet knife (a wide, bendy knife) to help it out. Put it on a serving plate once you have taken it out of the tin.

Place a sieve on top of a jug and empty the tin of peach slices into it. This will allow the syrup to drain into the jug, as you may be able to use some of it when mixing the jelly.

Place the peach slices, slightly overlapping each other, in a circle around the flan case. Then put the cherry in the middle. Follow the instructions on the jelly packet. About 5 minutes after you have made it you can pour it over the peaches. It should set quite quickly, but to speed it up you can put it in the fridge.

This will serve 4-6 people depending on the size of the slices you cut.

You would usually serve this with cream.

# APPLE PIE

**YOU NEED**

2-3 large cooking apples
4 dessertspoons sugar
200g (8 oz) self-raising flour
100g (4 oz) hard margarine or butter
1 egg

**TO MAKE**

Peel, core and slice the apples. Put them in a saucepan with enough water to cover the apples. Sprinkle on 2 dessertspoons of sugar. Put on a high heat to start with, and then turn down to simmer for 20 minutes.

To make a biscuit dough pastry, put the flour in a bowl and add the margarine or butter. Rub the fat into the flour using your fingers or a pastry maker (an enlarged semi-circle of 5 or 6 wires with a wooden handle).

Add the egg and 1 dessertspoonful of sugar. Press the pastry into a ball. Cut the ball in half. With one half, and a rolling pin rubbed in flour, put flour on the worktop. Roll out the pastry to cover the bottom half of a pie dish. Fit it over the dish and trim to fit with a knife. Remove the apples from the cooker and, using a sieve, drain the water out. If the apple has mixed with the water to become a pulp don't worry, you can still use it. It will just be a bit watery. Put the apple in the pie dish. Sprinkle another dessertspoonful of sugar over it. Roll out the rest of the pastry to cover the dish. Spread water round the bottom edge of pastry and put the lid on. Press all around the edge. Or you can decorate by pressing with a fork if you prefer. Trim the pastry round the edge of the pie. Prick the top a few times with a fork. Spread a thin layer of water over the top and sprinkle with a little sugar. Cook in the middle of the oven on gas mark 6 for 40 minutes. This should serve 4-6 people.

You would usually serve this with cream, ice cream or custard (see bread and butter pudding for custard).

# RICE PUDDING

**YOU NEED**

75g (3 oz) short grain rice
25g (1 oz) sugar
1 pint milk
Nutmeg (optional)

**TO MAKE**

Put the rice in an ovenproof dish. Add the milk and sugar and allow to stand for 15 minutes. Stir gently and then place in an oven, middle shelf, gas mark 2, for 30 minutes. Remove from the oven and stir. If you like nutmeg, this is the time to grate a little over the top. Put back in the oven for a further 1½ to 2 hours. Then it's ready to eat.
This will serve 2 people.
You would normally serve this with sugar, jam or golden syrup.

# BREAD AND BUTTER PUDDING

**YOU NEED**

6 slices of bread
Soft butter (enough to spread on the bread)
75g 3oz sultanas
75g 3oz currants
1 pint milk
2 tablespoons custard powder
1 tablespoon sugar

**TO MAKE**

First turn the oven on to gas mark 4 to warm it up. Use an oblong dish. Spread the bread with the butter on both sides, cut in half diagonally and place into the dish. Mix the currants and the sultanas and sprinkle some over one side of the bread. Place another slice of buttered bread on the top and sprinkle some more sultanas and currants on the top and continue until you have used all of the slices of bread. Add the milk to a saucepan and boil. Then add the custard powder and sugar to the milk and stir until it thickens.
Remove from the heat and put the saucepan onto a heatproof mat. Pour half of the custard on to the bread and fruit and leave to stand for 15 minutes to allow it to soak into the bread. Then add the rest of the custard.
Put into the oven for 20 to 25 minutes.
You can serve it with more custard, ice cream or cream.

# CUSTARD

**YOU NEED**

1 pint of milk
2 tablespoonfuls of custard powder
1 tablespoonful sugar

**TO MAKE**

Put the custard powder, sugar and a little of the milk into a large jug and blend together. The rest of the milk should be put in a saucepan and brought to the boil. When it boils, pour into the jug and mix everything together. Empty back into the saucepan on a medium heat. Stir constantly until the custard starts to boil. Then it's ready.

# APPLE AND BLACKBERRY CRUMBLE

**YOU NEED**

2 large cooking apples
200g (8 oz) blackberries
100g (4 oz) plain flour
50g (2 oz) hard margarine or butter
3 dessertspoonfuls sugar

**TO MAKE**

Peel, core and slice the apple into a saucepan. Put in enough water to cover the apples. Add the blackberries and 2 dessertspoons of sugar. Turn on to a high heat. Once it boils turn down to simmer for 20 minutes.

In another bowl, put the flour and margarine or butter. Rub together until breadcrumbs are made, either by hand or using a pastry maker. This is half an oval shaped made of about 5 wire strands and with a wooden, or plastic handle. Add the last dessertspoon of sugar to the crumble mixture.

Place a sieve over a jug and strain the water out of the apple and blackberries if possible. If not, you'll have to add them as they are. Put the fruit in a serving dish and sprinkle over the crumble mix. Cook in an oven, gas mark 5, on the middle shelf for 30-40 minutes. The top should be crispy.

This will serve 4 people and would normally be served with cream, ice cream or custard (see bread and butter pudding).

# BAKED APPLES

**YOU NEED**

4 large cooking apples
75g (3 oz) sultanas
50g (2 oz) soft brown sugar (or Demerara)

**TO MAKE**

Wash and core the apples. Place them on a baking tray. Then mix the sugar and sultanas. Push the mixture into the centre of the apples (where the core was). Bake in the oven on the middle shelf, gas mark 4, for three quarters of an hour.
This will serve 4 people.
You would normally serve it with cream, ice cream or custard.

# SYRUP SPONGE

**YOU NEED**

4 tablespoons of golden syrup
100g (4 oz) self-raising flour
100g (4 oz) caster sugar
100g (4 oz) soft margarine or soft butter
2 eggs
1 teaspoon vanilla essence

**TO MAKE**

Put the golden syrup in a large heatproof dish (about 2 pints size). Use your finger to help to get the syrup off the spoon. In another bowl, put the flour, sugar, margarine or soft butter, eggs and vanilla essence. Mix together well until thick and creamy. Place this sponge mixture on top of the syrup, making sure that the syrup is totally covered. Smooth the top of the sponge mixture to make the depth roughly equal all over. If you have a microwave, you can put it in for 5-7 minutes and then it should be cooked. The problem with microwave food is that the sponge will still be white, but if you have it with custard, you won't see it.

Alternatively, you can cook it in a steamer. Cover the top of the bowl with a piece of foil to make a lid. Then put a large pan of boiling water on the stove, placing a steamer on the top. Put the bowl in the steamer and turn the heat to simmer. You will need to check that the pan of water doesn't boil dry. Cook for about an hour and a half. This should serve 4 people and is best served with custard (see bread and butter pudding).

# CHERRY CHEESECAKE

**YOU NEED**

6 digestive biscuits
50g (2 oz) butter
300g (12 oz) full fat soft cream cheese
Tin of cherry topping OR
1 tin of cherries and 1 rounded teaspoon of arrowroot

**TO MAKE**

In a tin, place enough foil to cover the bottom and rise up the sides so that you will be able to lift it out when the time comes.

Put the biscuits in a plastic bag. Close the top and hold tight and roll with a rolling pin until the biscuit is made into crumbs. Put the butter on a low heat until it has melted. Turn off the heat. Add the biscuit crumbs and stir well until they are covered in butter. Press down the mixture in the tin (on top of the foil) and make it fairly smooth.

Place the cream cheese on top of this. If the cherries are in thick syrup or are a cherry topping, you can put them straight on the top. Put in the fridge for 30 minutes before eating.

You may prefer the cheese to be a little less fattening. In which case, you need to mix 1 packet of mascarpone cheese (or 100g (4 oz)) with 200g (8 oz) of fromage frais. Then replace the cream cheese in the recipe.

If you can only find cherries in juice, put them in a strainer or sieve over a saucepan. The juice will drain into the pan. Put the cherries on one side. Add 1 teaspoon of arrowroot and stir on a medium heat until it thickens. Turn off and return the cherries and allow it to go cold. It can then be put on top of the cheese.

This should serve 4-6 people.

# SHERRY TRIFLE

**YOU NEED**

1 small tin of strawberries
3 sponge fingers
Sherry
1 packet of red quick setting jelly
2 tablespoons custard powder
1 tablespoon sugar
1 pint of milk
Half pint pot of double or whipping cream
6 glace cherries

**TO MAKE**

Open the tin of strawberries and empty them into a sieve, which is above a jug. It may be that you can use the juice when making the jelly. Place the strawberries in the bottom of a large bowl or decorative dish. Break the finger sponges into 2 or 3 pieces. Spread them fairly evenly amongst the strawberries. Pour a little sherry over the sponges. Follow the instructions on the packet of quick setting jelly. Pour it over the strawberries and sponges. Leave this to set for 10 minutes.

Next, make the custard. In a large jug, put the custard powder and sugar. With a little of the milk, mix to make a liquid. Put the rest of the milk in a saucepan and turn the heat high to boil. When the boiling starts (starts to bubble and rise in the pan) turn off. Add the milk to the jug and stir. Return the contents to the saucepan on a medium heat. Stir constantly. When this starts to boil, turn the heat off. Leave to stand for 10 minutes to cool. Stir occasionally to prevent a skin forming. Then pour into the bowl on top of the jelly. Place in the fridge and leave to set. When the custard has set, put the cream into a jug or bowl. Whisk until it becomes stiff. Spread over the custard. Cut the glace cherries in half and use them to decorate the trifle. Return to the fridge until you are ready to eat it.

This will serve 4-6 people.

If you would prefer trifle without sherry, leave it out and the sponge fingers and make the same way.

# STRAWBERRY FOOL

**YOU NEED**

Half a kg (1lb) of strawberries
2 tablespoons sugar
1 teaspoon corn flour
Half a pint of milk
Half a pint of double or whipping cream

**TO MAKE**

In a large saucepan, put 1 tablespoon of sugar, the cornflour and a little milk. Mix well. Add the rest of the milk. Put on a medium heat. Stir constantly until it thickens. Turn off the heat and leave to go cold. Wash the strawberries and remove the green leaves on the top. Push through a sieve, but it will be quicker in a blender if you have one. Turn on the blender to puree the strawberries. If you use a blender, you will need to put them through a sieve afterwards anyway to remove any seeds.
In another bowl, put the cream. Whisk well until it thickens. Fold into the milk and strawberry puree. Place in glasses and hopefully you will still be able to get it in the fridge for 2 hours. This will serve 2-4 people.

# STRAWBERRY PANCAKES

**YOU NEED**

200g (8 oz) strawberries
2 teaspoons sugar
1 egg
3 rounded tablespoons plain flour
A pinch of salt
Half a pint of milk
7 tablespoons of oil
A small carton of double or whipping cream

**TO MAKE**

Wash the strawberries and remove any leaves. Cut them in half and put them in a bowl with the sugar. Place the cream in another bowl and whisk until stiff. You can use a balloon whisk – a metal whisk with open strands of metal, which will make your arm ache, or a mixer – which is a lot easier.
In a jug, put the flour, egg, salt and milk. Stir together well using a fork. It should be about the thickness of cream. If it's thicker, add a little water. You have then made the pancake mixture.
Put 4 tablespoons of oil in a frying pan. Turn the heat on to high. Pour in half the pancake mixture. Swirl the frying pan around so the pancake covers the bottom. When the pancake no longer has liquid on the top, it is time to turn it over. You can either do this using a fish slice or the brave can toss it. You will need to slide it to the edge of the pan before you try. When it is cooked put it on a serving plate.
Just to one side of the middle of the pancake put some strawberries and cream.
Roll the pancake up to cover the strawberries and cream.
Repeat the whole process again to make a second pancake.
This will serve 1-2 people.

# CAKES AND PASTRIES

# VICTORIA SPONGE

**YOU NEED**

2 x 18cm (7 inch) sandwich tins
100g (4 oz) self-raising flour
100g (4 oz) soft margarine
100g (4oz caster sugar
2 eggs
1 teaspoon vanilla essence
Strawberry jam
1 teaspoon icing sugar (optional)

**TO MAKE**

Grease the tins and sprinkle a little flour over them to stop a grease mark appearing on the cake. If you can only get 20cm (8 inch) tins, you will have to increase the 100g (4 oz) weights to 150g (6 oz).

In a mixing bowl put the flour, margarine, sugar, eggs and vanilla essence. Mix well until it's a creamy consistency. Divide between the two sandwich tins and smooth until roughly the same depth all over. Place on the middle shelf of the oven, gas mark 5, for 30 minutes. To check that it's cooked, gently press the middle of the sponge. If it's cooked it will spring back into place. If not, leave for a little longer. When it's cooked, remove from the tins and put on a cooling rack.

When cold, put the worst looking sponge upside down on a serving plate (with the flat surface at the top). Spread liberally with strawberry jam and put the other sponge on the top.

To give a more professional appearance, put the icing sugar in a tea strainer or a sieve over the cake. With a spoon rubbed over the surface sprinkle the icing sugar all over the top. This should serve 6 people.

# SMALL ICED CAKES

**YOU NEED**

A cake tray with 12 places
A cake tray with 6 places
Cake cases
100g (4 oz) self-raising flour
100g (4 oz) caster sugar
100g (4 oz) soft margarine
2 eggs
1 teaspoon vanilla essence
100g (4 oz) icing sugar
9 glace cherries

**TO MAKE**

Place the cake cases in the cake trays. In a mixing bowl put the flour, sugar, margarine, eggs and vanilla essence. Stir or whisk well until it is a creamy consistency. Put a large teaspoonful of the mixture into the cake cases. If you have any left try to divide it equally between the cases. Cook in the oven, gas mark 5, middle shelf for about 25 minutes. When cooked remove from the oven and put on a cooling rack.

When the cakes are cold, cut the cherries in half. Put the icing sugar in a bowl. Add 2 teaspoons of water and mix well. It should make a soft, thick consistency. If it's too thick and will not be able to spread, add extra water half a teaspoon at a time. You will need to find a suitable consistency because you don't want it too runny either. Spread a little in the middle of the cakes and put half a cherry on the top.

If you wish you can put different things on the top, like chocolate buttons, smarties or sugar strands (hundreds and thousands).

To change the flavour completely you can leave out the vanilla essence and add finely grated rind of lemon or lemon essence and orange and sugared lemon or orange slices on the top.

This should make up to 18 cakes.

# SULTANA CAKE

**YOU NEED**

20cm (8 inch) round cake tin
Greaseproof paper
200g (8 oz) sultanas
200g (8 oz) self-raising flour
100g (4 oz) soft margarine
100g (4 oz) caster sugar
2 eggs
1 teaspoon vanilla essence

**TO MAKE**

First you will need to line the tin with greaseproof paper, put the tin on the paper and draw around it. Cut out the circle and put to one side. The sides will need to be 2cm (half an inch) deeper than the side of the tin. It will probably need two pieces of paper, which should overlap to make sure the tin is properly covered. When you have cut the paper, fold over the extra 2cm (half an inch) and snip down to the fold. You only need to cut about 3cm (1 inch) apart to make it fold around the tin. Place the sides into the tin followed by the bottom.
In a bowl, put the flour, margarine, sugar, eggs and vanilla essence. Mix well to a thick, creamy consistency. Fold in the sultanas. Put the mixture into the cake tin. Smooth the top lightly. Place on the middle shelf of the oven. Gas mark 5 for 1 hour. To check to see if it's cooked, stick a skewer in the centre of the cake. If it's clean when you remove it, it's cooked. If there is a little cake mixture left on it, it needs cooking a little longer. I would try it every 10 minutes, but it shouldn't need much longer.
This will make 6-8 slices.

# MADEIRA CAKE

**YOU NEED**

A 20cm (8 inch) round cake tin
Greaseproof paper
200g (8 oz) self-raising flour
200g (8 oz) caster sugar
100g (4 oz) soft margarine
2 eggs
1 teaspoon vanilla essence

**TO MAKE**

First you need to line the cake tin. Put the tin on some greaseproof paper. Draw around it. Cut the circle out and leave on one side for now. Next you need to make the sides. You will probably have to use 2 pieces of paper. Make sure they will overlap. Make them the depth of the sides of the tin plus 2cm (half an inch) Fold over the short extra piece of paper and snip down to the fold – about every 3cm (or inch). Then put the sides into the tin – snipped edge first, and then the round bottom piece.
In a bowl, put all the ingredients. Mix well until it is thick and creamy. Spoon into the tin and smooth the top fairly level.
Put in the oven on gas mark 4 for 1 hour. This should make 6 slices.

# MELTING MOMENTS

**YOU NEED**

125g (5 oz) self-raising flour
75g (3 oz) hard margarine
75g (3 oz) caster sugar
Half an egg
Pinch of salt
75g (3 oz) oats
3 glace cherries

**TO MAKE**

Put the flour and margarine into a bowl. Rub the margarine into the flour to make breadcrumbs. Add the caster sugar and salt. Break an egg into a cup and mix well with a fork. Add half the egg to the flour mixture and stir well. Tip the oats on to the worktop. Divide the mixture into 6 and roll into balls in the oats. Cut the cherries in half and place half a cherry on each ball. Place the balls on a large baking tray, not too close together to cook. Press the balls down slightly as you put them on, to ensure they don't roll away.
Cook on the middle shelf of the oven. Gas mark 4 for 15 minutes.
This should make 6 melting moments.

# FRUIT SCONES

**YOU NEED**

A large pastry cutter (usually round)
200g (8 oz) self-rising flour
50g (2 oz) hard margarine
50g (2 oz) caster sugar
75g (3 oz) sultanas
A quarter of a pint of milk
Pinch of salt

**TO MAKE**

In a bowl put the flour and margarine. Rub the margarine into the flour with your fingertips until it resembles breadcrumbs. Add the sugar, salt and sultanas. Mix in the milk and knead well. Flatten the dough a little and, with the pastry cutter, cut out the scones. If you don't have a pastry cutter you can make square ones or use a cup.
Put them on a baking tray, just above the middle of the oven, gas mark 6, for 10 minutes.
This will make about 6 scones.
To make cheese scones, leave out the sultanas and sugar and add 75g (3 oz) of grated cheese.
To make plain scones, just leave out the sultanas and sugar.

# CHOCOLATE CRISPIE CAKES

**YOU NEED**

A 12-space cake tray
Cake cases
50g (2 oz) cooking chocolate
Rice crispies

**TO MAKE**

Put the cake cases in the tray. Break the chocolate up and put in a 2-pint ovenproof dish. Melt the chocolate either by putting it in a microwave for one and a half minutes or in steam over a pan of boiling water until it has melted.
Fill the dish two thirds full with rice crispies and stir well with a metal spoon. Make sure all the crispies are covered in chocolate. Spoon the crispies into the cake cases, using a teaspoon. Any that is left or if all the cases haven't been used, just spread it amongst the cases filled. Leave on one side to set for about half an hour. If it's too warm you'll need to put them in the fridge.
You can use cornflakes or branflakes instead of rice crispies if you prefer. This will make up to 12 cakes.

# FLAPJACK

**YOU NEED**

200g (8 oz) porridge oats
100g (4 oz) hard margarine
50g (2 oz) sugar – preferably Demerara
1 tablespoon of golden syrup
Pinch of salt

**TO MAKE**

In a large saucepan, put the margarine, sugar and golden syrup. Turn the gas to a low heat. When it has dissolved remove the pan from the heat and stir in the oats. Scrape into a square or oblong heatproof container. Place in the oven, middle shelf, gas mark 4, for 20 minutes. When cooked remove from the oven and place on a heatproof mat to go cold. Slice in half then cut into slices.
You can make raisin flapjack by adding 75g (3 oz) raisins.
Crispy flapjack can be made by adding 50g (2 oz) crumbled cornflakes. You can crush them in your hand.
The amount it makes really depends on how big you cut the slices.

# CHOCOLATE BROWNIES

**YOU NEED**

100g (4 oz) butter
100g (4 oz) cooking chocolate
100g (4 oz) dark brown sugar
100g (4 oz) self-raising flour
2 eggs
2 teaspoons of cocoa powder
1 teaspoon of vanilla essence
Pinch of salt
100g (4 oz) chopped nuts (optional) OR
Chocolate chips (optional)
A dish approximately 18 x 23 cm (7 x 9 inches)

**TO MAKE**

Grease the dish well. In a 2 pint bowl put the broken up chocolate and the butter. Put in a steamer over a saucepan of boiling water on a low heat. When this has melted, remove from the heat and stir in all the other ingredients (except the nuts or chocolate chips). Stir until it is a smooth consistency. Add the nuts or chocolate chips if desired. Put in the dish and cook in the middle of the oven, gas mark 4 for 30 minutes. Remove from the oven and leave to stand until cold. Cut into slices.
The amount you make will depend on the size of your slices.
You can make these in a microwave oven. Just put the chocolate and butter in a large bowl. Place in the microwave oven for 40 seconds, which should melt them. Remove from the oven and mix in everything but the nuts or chocolate chips. Add them last. Scrape the mixture into the dish and cook in the microwave for 4-5 minutes. Leave on one side to cool, then cut into slices as normal.

# APPLE TURNOVER

**YOU NEED**

1 packet of puff pastry
2 large cooking apples
3 dessertspoons of sugar

**TO MAKE**

Thaw the pastry.
Peel, core and slice the apples into a saucepan. Add 2 dessertspoons of sugar and enough water to cover the apples. Put on a high heat to bring to the boil, then turn down to simmer for 20 minutes.
Sprinkle some flour on the worktop. Rub some flour onto the rolling pin. Place the pastry on the worktop and roll out to about 30cm (12 inches) square. You should put flour on the rolling pin to stop the pastry sticking. Cut the pastry in half lengthways, then sideways to make 4 squares of pastry
If the apple has finished cooking, put it in a sieve to drain off the water. Put a spoonful of apple in the centre of the square of pastry. You are going to fold the pastry to make a triangle, so you can add a little more apple if you think there will be space. With a pastry brush, brush water on the edges of the pastry, which are to join together. Press gently to fix it properly. Tap the edges you have stuck together with the back of a knife to help it to flake. Prick the top with a fork to let any excess steam out. Brush the top of the triangle with water and sprinkle with sugar. Place on a tray and put in the oven, just above the middle shelf, gas mark 6, for 25-30 minutes. Remove from the oven when cooked and put on a cooling rack until cold.
If you want to, you can put some cream, whisked until stiff, into the joined side of the triangle, which has been sliced.
This will make 4 turnovers.

# JAM TARTS

**YOU NEED**

A 12-space cake tray
A 6-space cake tray
A large round pastry cutter
200g (8 oz) plain flour
100g (4 oz) hard margarine or butter
A pinch of salt
Jam

**TO MAKE**

Put the flour, margarine or butter and salt in a bowl. Rub the margarine or butter into the flour to make breadcrumbs. Add 1 tablespoon of water. Try to make the breadcrumbs into a ball. If you can't, add extra water 1 dessertspoon at a time. Too much water will make the pastry hard, too little and it will be impossible to work with. Once you have made the pastry ball, sprinkle the worktop with flour and put the pastry in the middle. Rub flour on the rolling pin and roll the pastry to about 3mm (an eighth of an inch) thick. Using the pastry cutter cut out circles. Place the circles in the spaces on the cake tray. Any pastry left over should be made into a ball and rolled out again. Put a generous teaspoon of jam into each pastry circle.

Put the trays into the oven, just above the middle shelf, gas mark 6, for 25-30 minutes. When you remove them, you would probably be best to put them on a mat to cool down for 5 minutes before taking them out of the tray with a pallet knife (a large flexible knife) and placing on a cooling rack.

This should make up to 18 jam tarts.

If for any reason you have any pastry left you can put it in a plastic bag in the freezer for later use.

# MINCE PIES

**YOU NEED**

A 12-space cake tray
A 6-space cake tray
Small and large pastry cutters
200g (8 oz) self-raising flour
100g (4 oz) hard margarine or butter
1 egg
2 dessertspoons of sugar
Mincemeat

**TO MAKE**

Traditionally shortcrust pastry is used to make mince pies (see Jam Tarts), but as I prefer biscuit crust, I'm afraid that's the recipe I will use.

In a bowl put the flour, salt and margarine or butter. Rub the fat into the flour so that it looks like breadcrumbs.

In a cup or mug, break the egg. Whisk with a fork. Add the egg and sugar to the flour and make into a ball using your fingers. Sprinkle flour onto the worktop and put the pastry ball on it. Rub flour on to the rolling pin and roll out the pastry until it is about 3mm (an eighth of an inch) thick. Cut it into circles with the pastry cutter. You will need a small and a large one for each pie.

Place the large pastry circles in the spaces on the cake tray. Put a teaspoonful of mincemeat in each one. Using a pastry brush, brush water around the edge of the circle, just above the mincemeat. Cover with the small circle and gently push into place. Prick with a fork. You will probably find it easier to do the same stage with a lot of pies at the same time. You may also find that you do not have enough pastry to make 18, so don't put any mincemeat in until you have made the top.

You can put them all in the oven together, just above the middle, gas mark 6, for about 25-30 minutes.

When removing them from the oven, first put them on a mat for 5 minutes to cool down. Then remove them with a palette knife (a wide flexible knife) onto a cooling rack. When they're cool, with the help of a tea strainer or a sieve, sprinkle a little icing sugar over them for a finishing touch. This should make up to 18.